Pupil Friendly
Individual Education Plans

For pupils and students aged 6 to 16

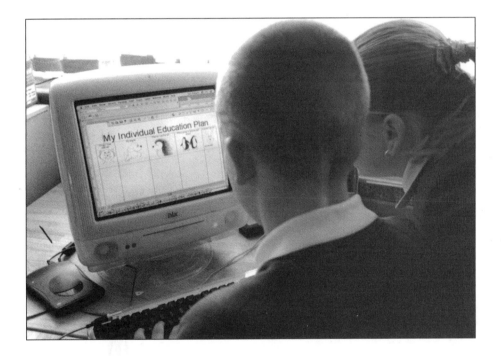

Gillian Shotton
Educational Psychologist

Lucky Duck is more than a publishing house and training agency. George Robinson and Barbara Maines founded the company in the 1980s when they worked together as a head and psychologist developing innovative strategies to support challenging students.

They have an international reputation for their work on bullying, self-esteem, emotional literacy and many other subjects of interest to the world of education.

George and Barbara have set up a regular news-spot on the website. Twice yearly these items will be printed as a newsletter. If you would like to be put on the mailing list to receive this then please contact us:

e-mail newsletter@luckyduck.co.uk   website www.luckyduck.co.uk

ISBN 1 904 315 04 6

Published by Lucky Duck Publishing Ltd

www.luckyduck.co.uk

Commissioning Editor: George Robinson
Editor: Mel Maines
Designer: Helen Weller

Original illustrations by Gillian Shotton

Printed by Antony Rowe Limited

© Gillian Shotton 2003

Second edition including material for older students published 2004 with additional illustrations by Mike Cadman and Owen Knowles.

Contents

Acknowledgements

To Keith, for being such a support and encouragement. Also thanks to Hilary Robbins (Assistant Principal Educational Psychologist, Hampshire) and Sheila Burton (Senior Educational Psychologist, Hampshire) for their useful comments and suggestions.

Introduction

Children who are capable of forming views, have a right to receive and make known information, to express an opinion and to have that opinion taken into account in any matters affecting them. The views of the child should be given due weight according to the age, maturity and capability of the child.

From Articles 12 and 13, The United Nations Convention on the Rights of the Child as set out in the Code of Practice for SEN (2001).

Traditionally, completing Individual Education Plans (IEPs) has been a task that teachers have often done without involving pupils. The writing and reviewing of plans in this way does have some value. It helps teachers to think about the targets they are expecting a pupil to achieve as well as plan and review strategies. It struck me a number of years ago, however, that this process, even when it actively involved the parents, was missing someone rather important out of the equation – the pupil!

Can you imagine what it must be like to have someone decide that you are not doing so well in a particular area, make up some targets for you behind your back and then, at a future date, evaluate you on those targets? The audacity! Some children might also be outraged, thinking, "How dare they? They might have told me if they thought I wasn't doing so well. Had I known what my targets were, or at least had some discussion about making them up, I would have been more motivated to achieve them." Other children may not be so bothered that their teachers have left them out of the process. However, being left out further reinforces their lack of motivation and does nothing to encourage them to start to take some responsibility for their own learning. Yet it is still commonplace to find that pupils have not been involved in the writing of their IEPs. The OFSTED review (1999) of the old Code of Practice for SEN, stated that a common weakness in IEPs was a lack of pupil involvement.

Pupils often have no idea that they even have targets, let alone have a copy of them. Where pupils have been told about their targets and had them written down, they have often not been involved in the construction of those targets and, in fact, have little motivation to achieve them. Is it any wonder then that they do not make the progress hoped for? The new Code of Practice (2001) makes it very clear that pupils should be involved in planning their targets from an early age:

"Children should, where possible, participate in all the decision making processes that occur in education, including the setting of learning targets and contributing to IEPs."   **Paragraph 3.2**

"From an early age pupils with SEN should be actively involved at an appropriate level in discussions about their IEPs, including target setting and review arrangements, and have their views recorded."   **Paragraph 3.9**

"Pupils with special educational needs should become progressively more involved in setting and evaluating targets within the IEP process...actively encouraging these pupils to track their own progress and record achievement within a programme action designed to meet their particular learning or behavioural difficulty will contribute to improved confidence and self image." **Paragraph 3.14**

Using the IEPs in this book will help teachers to involve pupils in the planning of them. Because they are attractive and written in pupil–friendly language, the format can be easily understood. The IEPs give the ownership of the targets back to the child and because there are a variety of designs to choose from, children really enjoy the process of selecting one that suits their interests. They enjoy constructing their plan in partnership with an adult. Whether using the photocopiable masters or working with the child to write their plan straight onto the computer, I hope that teachers will enjoy this process, as it provides the opportunity to have an interesting, positive and purposeful conversation with the pupil.

The guide gives further reasons for involving pupils in this way as well as some practical tips and guidance for writing IEPs in partnership with the child. At the back you will find two examples of IEPs written in this way to give a flavour of how a completed IEP might look.

Finding the time

As teachers will be involving the child in the writing process, the only time they are going to be able to do this is when the child is in school, i.e. during school hours. In schools where this approach has been used successfully, the SENCO or Head has been able to provide teaching staff with non-contact time in order to have individual sessions with each child in turn. Teachers, as well as pupils, have found this a valuable and rewarding experience. So, rather than putting teachers under pressure, by asking them to do more paperwork in their non-contact time, the approach takes the pressure off teaching staff and allows the whole process of filling in IEPs to be much more meaningful. For this to happen, the approach needs to be given the priority it deserves by senior management, as release time needs to be arranged. There are obviously time and cost implications attached to this. The question then comes down to values. Does the school really value the pupil being involved in the making of their IEP? If they do, they will find a way to do it. Where there is a will…

Why involve the child?

It is their right to be involved

The 1989 United Nations Convention of the Rights of the Child states in Article 12 that children who are capable of forming their own views shall have the right 'to express those views freely in all matters' affecting them and that their views should be given 'due weight in accordance with the age and maturity of the child'. It also states that all children should be provided with the opportunity to be heard in any proceedings affecting them. In Article 13 it states that children should have the right to express their views, 'receive and impart information and ideas…regardless of frontiers, either orally or in writing… or through any other media of the child's choice'. Clearly, there is a legislative context for involving children in the making of their IEPs, as of course their IEPs are most definitely matters affecting them.

Improved self-esteem

Personally, I achieve more and feel better about myself when I feel involved and have some degree of control. It helps when I know what I'm trying to achieve, by when and who/what is going to help me. I need to own the learning targets rather than them being something that I perceive someone is trying to force on me. I'm sure that if you reflect on positive learning experiences in your own life you will share similar thoughts. It is vital for many children, who may already feel pretty poor about themselves and how they are doing in school, to feel that they have some degree of control with regard to their learning or behaviour. If we help them to become involved in planning their targets with them, it will help them to feel better about themselves, showing them that their views really do count. Through regularly reviewing their targets with them, they will be able to see that they can make progress, which will also help them to feel better about themselves.

Research evidence

Research evidence shows that children themselves state a preference for being involved. Brennan (1988) investigated pupils' attitudes towards Records of Achievement (ROA – an interactive model of record keeping involving pupils and teachers). Pupils liked the system and reported the following benefits:

- ▶ a greater feeling of involvement and motivation to work
- ▶ a greater feeling of responsibility for their own progress
- ▶ a greater pride in their achievements.

All of these are intrinsically linked with pupil motivation, perception of control, confidence and empowerment.

Feedback

Involving children presents them with an opportunity to reflect on their learning and encourages them to take more of an active role in planning and reviewing their progress. Subsequently, pupils will be in a position to offer feedback on teaching and learning styles and the curriculum on offer. Reviewing what did not go quite so well, in terms of meeting targets, can be enlightening and can help everyone involved in making the necessary adjustments for next time. For example, Justin, a year four pupil, had only managed to learn a quarter of the words specified on his IEP for spelling. In reviewing his IEP with him, he expressed some frustration. "I do learn my spellings every week," he outlined, "I mostly get them right each week, but when I learn the ones for the following week, I forget the other ones I've learnt!" With this information, his teacher was able to adjust his weekly spelling list to allow some over-learning and revision of spellings he had previously forgotten. He subsequently managed to learn and retain many more.

A word of caution

Although it is important to involve children as fully as possible we must be careful not to overburden them.

"There is a fine balance between giving children a voice and overburdening them with decision making procedures where they have insufficient experience and knowledge to make an appropriate judgement without additional support." (The Children Act 1989, Guidance and regulations, DOH 1991, Vol. 6, 6.6.)

In practice, this means using our professional judgement to give children as much help and guidance as they need in making their IEPs. The amount we give will of course depend on the age and maturity of the child as well as their attention span.

How to use the pupil friendly Individual Education Plans

1. Work out some targets in rough before sitting down with the pupil

Before actually sitting down with the pupil to write their IEP you need to have first spent some time thinking about their particular areas of need and jotting down in rough what their targets might look like. This is also the time to consult other relevant information you have available, such as the results from any recent assessments as well as the pupil's particular strengths and learning style (e.g. Jack seems to learn best when I present things more visually). The SMART acronym is useful for writing effective targets, i.e. ask yourself, are the targets...

Specific? (e.g. learn to spell three words each week)

Measurable? (e.g. can spelling be checked in written work/test conditions?)

Achievable? (given time and support at home and school)

Relevant? (e.g. words that the pupil will want to use)

Timed? (e.g. for six weeks)

The SEN Toolkit, section 5, page 7

If you do not plan some targets in advance, before you start to talk with the pupil, you may find yourself too distracted to be able to come up with SMART targets when you have the pupil actually sitting next to you. The targets that you both write together may not be the exact ones you originally planned, but at least you will have thought through where you feel the pupil should be going next and what SMART targets might look like for him or her. You are going to be flexible enough to modify these targets later, so that the pupil's motivation is taken into account. For example, for one year three girl with literacy difficulties, I had originally jotted down that a good target would be if she could recognise three key words each week for the next six weeks. When I sat down with her to write the IEP she was absolutely convinced that she would be able to learn five per week. Thinking to myself, "Well that's probably a bit ambitious," we wrote the target as being five words per week. After six weeks I found that she had indeed achieved her target. "See I told you I could do it!" she proudly informed me. She had taken ownership of the goal and was consequently motivated to achieve it.

Depending on the age of the pupil, it is usually better to plan just two or three targets. This ties in with the new Code of Practice for SEN, which advocates using a limited number of targets (3-4) rather than many, which no-one can remember anyway. It outlines that the targets should relate to the key areas of communication, literacy, numeracy and behaviour/social skills. The SEN Toolkit (section 5: Managing IEPs, paragraph 8) also helpfully adds that the IEP targets should be limited to current agreed priorities for the pupil.

2. Setting up the materials and the environment

a. Writing the targets with the child directly onto the computer

> I have found it to be very effective to sit down with the pupil at the computer in order to write his/her IEP. The IEPs on the disc are in Microsoft Word, which most schools use. Insert the CD-ROM then go into Word. Select file, select open, then select the D: drive from the scroll down box where it says 'look in'. The computer will show you the files contained on the CD-ROM, i.e. the dinosaur IEP, the fish IEP, the football IEP and the animal IEP. Open up each document so you are ready to present the alternative designs to the pupil for them to choose between on screen. Alternatively you could print out the different IEPs for the pupil to make a selection.

> Young people love to see their words translated into print on the screen and then to receive a colour printout to take home for their bedroom wall. An added advantage of having the IEP on the computer is that you do not have to write the whole thing out all over again when you come to review and change the targets. You need to use a computer in a quiet location where you and the pupil can have some privacy.

b. Using the photocopiable masters

> If your IT skills are not up to it, or you do not have a computer with a colour printer in a suitable location, you can use the photocopiable formats. Here again you will need to have ready the four different IEP designs for the pupil to choose between. After the IEP is written you can take a photocopy whilst the pupil takes the original. Another possibility is for an administrative person or support assistant to type up the hand written version so that a typed colour printout can be obtained.

> Another option is to laminate the IEP before writing it and then use a non water-soluble fine tipped OHP pen to write it. Once written, it can be photocopied with the pupil retaining the colour laminated version. The advantage of laminating is that the IEP can be revised by wiping off some of the information without having to rewrite the whole thing.

> Make sure the environment feels safe and secure for the pupil to feel at ease in. A quiet area, where they are not going to feel self-conscious because others can overhear, is important.

3. Explaining what the session is all about

A few suggested phrases…

> "We're going to spend some time making a plan together to help you learn even more, or to help you get more out of school/enjoy school even more, etc."

(Whatever is most relevant.) The pupil may need some reassurance that it is not because they've done anything wrong. At this point, show them the different IEP formats and ask which one they would like.

Before getting down to the actual writing of the plan it is helpful to have a more general conversation with the pupil, finding out more about their views.

The conversation might go something like this…

> "Before we write your plan together I want to find out a bit more about you and what you think, because what you think is important. Did you know that? I'm going to write down what you say to help me remember."

Finding out the answers to the following questions can be very enlightening:

- What do you think you are good at in school?
- What do you think you are not so good at in school?
- What is your favourite activity in school?
- What do you not like doing in school?
- Is there anything you're worried about at the moment?
- If you could choose just one thing to get better at in school this term, what would it be?

Finding out about what they would like to get better at is extremely valuable, as they will be much more likely to achieve their IEP targets if they are motivated.

4. Writing the plan together

Taking the format they have chosen, talk with them about the various headings in the plan, i.e. things I find difficult, my targets etc.

Then start to fill in the plan, section by section, moving across the page rather than down the columns. The following example shows how the conversation might run for each of the various sections.

Things I find difficult

> "Well, one thing you have already said that you find difficult is concentrating during the Literacy Hour. So what shall we put in this section?"

> "Staying focused on my work in science lessons because I don't understand the experiments." (Teacher/pupil writes this in.)

My targets

By negotiating the targets with the pupil, you ensure that the targets created are perceived by the pupil as being achievable. Involving the pupil in the process also ensures that the targets are going to be much more relevant to them.

"How would you like to learn better in the Literacy Hour/science lesson?"

"I'd like to be able to concentrate better."

Making the target timed

"How long do you think you can try and concentrate for each literacy session/science lesson without distracting anyone?"

"I'm not sure, 20 minutes maybe."

"Well let's start with 15 and see how you go, what do you think?"

"OK."

"So what shall we write in the section under 'My Targets'?"

"To try and stay focused on my work for 15 minutes."

Try to get the pupil to refine their targets to make them more specific

"The first half when you're all together, or the second half when you've got to do more individual work?"

"Second half, I'm OK in the first half."

"Great, so it's to stay focused on my work for 15 minutes in the second half of the session?"

"Yeah, every day."

Often you find that when the area of difficulty is a broad one, the pupil tends to make targets that are not easy to measure. Pupils often give targets such as 'to be good', 'to behave' or 'to concentrate'. They need some help unpacking what 'being good' or 'concentrating' actually means in practice. A useful question to ask is, "If I were to video you in your class and you were 'concentrating' what would I see you doing? What would I hear?"

"If I were to come into your class and video you during the second half of the Literacy Hour/science lesson and you were staying focused on your work, what would I see you doing?"

"I'd be sitting at my desk writing or looking at my work. I wouldn't be talking to anyone or touching them or anything."

"That's brilliant. So shall we use that as the target? So it's…"

"To sit at my desk and stay looking at my work – writing or thinking."

"For 15 minutes during the second half of the Literacy Hour/science lesson."

"Yeah." (Teacher/pupil writes this in.)

What do I need to do?

"Right, next section. What do you need to do in order to stay focused on your work when you're about to get started? When do you concentrate best? What helps you to stay focused?"

"Well, when I sit next to Richard I concentrate better because he always gets on with his work and that makes me get on with mine."

"OK, so what are we going to write here?"

"Sit next to Richard."

"Anything else?"

"Don't sit next to Ian, he puts me off and wants to talk all the time. I never get anything done when he's sitting nearby. Then I get into trouble."

"OK, so what shall we write?"

"Sit away from Ian and near the front." (Teacher/pupil writes this in.)

Who's going to help me and when?

"So, next section, 'Who's going to help me and when?' How can I help you to meet your target?"

"Don't know."

"Well, one idea is that we make a chart and every time you manage to concentrate for the 15 minutes, you colour in a block on the chart. At the end of the week, if you've done really well, you can take it home to show mum. Would that help do you think?"

"Yes."

"So, what shall I put here?" (Teacher/pupil writes in the phrase spoken by the pupil.)

Others may also be able to support the pupil in their plan, e.g. other pupils or parents/carers.

> Having completed the process for one target, start again at the first column jointly writing the IEP as before to create further targets. If carrying out this process at the computer, I usually do the typing because pupils' word processing skills tend to be too slow. Depending on the speed and legibility of their handwriting you might like to scribe for the pupil, if a handwritten IEP is being produced. Try to ensure that you use their own words as much as possible so that it remains theirs, even if you have a much more eloquent phrase in mind.

Review date

> "Now, last section, we just need to plan when we're going to look at how you are getting on with this plan and see if we need to change anything." (Write in the appropriate date.)

Make sure it is also written into your diary. Think practically about when you might be able to carry out this review session. The actual column remains blank at this stage, the idea being that you write the results of the review into the column. The Code of Practice advocates that IEPs should be reviewed at least twice per year and ideally termly or more frequently for some young people. At least one review should coincide with a routine parents'/carers' evening (paragraph 5.53).

Involving parents/carers

Once the plan has been written, it is important to invite the parents/carers into school to discuss it with them. I often ask the pupil to explain their plan to their parents/carers. This is a good way of checking out their understanding of the plan as well as helping them to take full ownership of it. Parents/carers often like to suggest how they can support their pupil to meet his/her targets. For example, taking them to McDonalds seems to be a common reward for targets met during the week. Rewards and help such as this can be written into the 'Who's going to help me and when?' section. Parents/carers should also be given a copy of the plan. This is often a good time to get everyone who has been involved to sign the plan at the appropriate section. Parents/carers really value being involved and plans that involve the parents/carers as well as the pupil are much more likely to succeed. The plan then feels like everyone is coming together to help support the pupil.

A script for writing an IEP for learning with a pupil

Introduction

"We're going to spend some time making a plan together to help you learn even more, or to help you get more out of school/enjoy school even more, etc."

Finding out about them

"Before we write your plan together I want to find out a bit more about you and what you think, because what you think is important. Did you know that? So I'm going to write down what you say to help me remember."

Useful questions

▸ What do you think you are good at in school?

▸ What do you think you are not so good at in school?

▸ What is your favourite activity in school?

▸ What do you not like doing in school?

▸ Who are your friends in school?

▸ What do you like doing at home?

▸ Is there anything you're worried about at the moment?

▸ If you could choose just one thing to get better at in school this term, what would it be?

Writing the IEP

Things I find difficult

"Well, the two things you said that you find difficult are reading and spelling. So what shall we put in this section?"

"Reading and spelling words." (Teacher/pupil writes this in.)

My targets

"How would you like to get better with your reading and spelling?"

"I'd like to be able to read and write more words like Susan can, without having to ask all the time."

"OK. How many words do you think you can learn each week?"

"I'm not sure, 5 maybe."

"Well let's start with 3 and see how you go, what do you think?"

"OK."

"So what shall we write in the section under 'My Targets'?"

"To learn to read and spell 3 words each week."

"And we'll try to do this for the next half term – so, for the next six weeks."

"OK."

"So, that will be all the words on your sheet." (Teacher circles or indicates these words.)

> Actually specifying the words on the IEP, or having a sheet of words attached, makes it easier for everyone (teachers, parents, carers LSAs and the pupil) to know exactly which words they are going to be working on.

What do I need to do?

"Right, next section, 'What do I need to do?' What do you need to do in order to learn your three words each week?"

"Well, it helps if I read my book to mum every day."

"Did it help to play those word games with Mrs Stanton?"

"Yeah, I like playing games."

"So what are we going to write here about what you need to do?"

"Learn 3 words per week. When I get home I will either read my book to mum or play a game that will help me learn my words for that week." (Teacher/pupil writes this in.)

Who's going to help me and when?

"So next section, 'Who's going to help me and when?' How can we help you in school to meet your target?"

"Don't know."

"Well, you said it helped when Mrs Stanton played those games with you, we could do that."

"OK."

"Does it help if you can see your words in the classroom?"

"Like near my desk? Yes it does, then I can remember them better."

"Great, I'll make a special poster then."

"And it helped me when dad put my words on the back of the toilet door to help me learn them."

"OK, so what shall we write here?" (Teacher/pupil writes in the phrase spoken by the pupil.)

> Having completed the process for one target, a further target or two can be created in a similar way.

Review date

"Now last section, we just need to plan when we're going to look at how you are getting on with this plan and see if we need to change anything." (Write in the appropriate date.)

The completed IEP can be found in Appendix A.

"Well done, you've worked really hard on this and thought a lot to make a really good plan. Your mum/dad/carer is coming in after school. I'd like you to show him/her the plan and explain to him/her what it is all about. Don't worry we'll do it together, OK?"

A script for writing an IEP for behaviour with a pupil

Introduction

"We're going to spend some time making a plan together to help you get more out of school/enjoy school even more etc."

Finding out about them

"Before we write your plan together I want to find out a bit more about you and what you think, because what you think is important. Did you know that? So I'm going to write down what you say to help me remember."

Some useful questions

▶ What do you think you are good at in school?

▶ What do you think you are not so good at in school?

▶ What is your favourite activity in school?

▶ What do you not like doing in school?

▶ Who are your friends in school?

▶ Do you usually have people to play with/hang out with at break time?

▶ Is there anything you're worried about at the moment?

▶ If you could choose just one thing to get better at in school this term, what would it be?

Writing the IEP

Things I find difficult

"Something you said before that you find difficult is working with other people without hitting them. So what shall we put in this section?"

"Working with other people without hitting." (Teacher/pupil writes this in.)

My Targets

"How would you like to get better at this?"

"I just get so frustrated, but I want to be able to work with Sam and Matthew because I do like it when we work together."

"OK, how long do you think you could work with them without getting frustrated and then doing something you might regret?"

"I'm not sure, half an hour maybe."

"Well let's start with 20 minutes and see how you go, what do you think?"

"OK."

"What shall we write in the section under 'My Targets'?"

"To work with Sam and Matthew for 20 minutes, be nice to them, listen to them and not hit them."

"OK."

"How many times a week do you think you can do that?"

"Not sure, a few times maybe."

"OK, shall we put three for now?"

"Yeah." (Teacher/pupil writes in the full target.)

What do I need to do?

"Next section, 'What do I need to do?' What do you need to do in order to work well with Sam and Matthew and not hit them? What helps you to calm down when you start to feel angry and frustrated?"

"Well, it helps if I just go off by myself and look at a book for a bit."

"OK, let's write that in here, what shall I write?" (Teacher/pupil writes it in.)

Who's going to help me and when?

"So next section, 'Who's going to help me and when?' How can we help you in school to meet your target?"

"Don't know."

"Well, you said it helped when Mrs Stanton worked with you, Sam and Matthew."

"Yeah, its much easier to get on with them when she's there."

"Is there something you could get if you manage to work well for the 20 minutes?"

"Could I get one of those really cool stickers you've got?"

"That's a good idea. I'm sure we can give you one of those and we could put it on a special chart."

"Yeah."

"OK, so what shall we write here?" (Teacher/pupil writes in the phrase spoken by the pupil.)

Having completed the process for one target, further targets can be created in the same way.

Review date

"Now last section, we just need to plan when we're going to look at how you are getting on with this plan and see if we need to change anything." (Write in the appropriate date.)

The completed IEP can be found in Appendix B.

"Well done, you've worked really hard on this and thought a lot to make a really good plan. Your mum/dad/carer is coming in after school. I'd like you to show him/her the plan and explain to him/her what it is all about. Don't worry, we'll do it together."

Helping pupils see their progress

Once the IEP has been written, everyone's motivation will be at a high level. However, it is easy for that motivation to tail off unless the pupil has regular feedback on their progress. There are lots of ways to get pupils more actively involved in monitoring their progress on a more regular basis. 'Self-Esteem: A Classroom Affair' by Michele and Craig Borba has some great ideas, a few of which I have adapted here. Charts, tapes, books and folders are also great motivators for pupils to take home and share with their parents/carers on how well they are doing. Parents/carers also appreciate this type of regular positive feedback.

Charts

Words I can read and spell

Colour the words you can read and spell

My Spelling Tests

Colour or decorate the number of words you spelled correctly this week

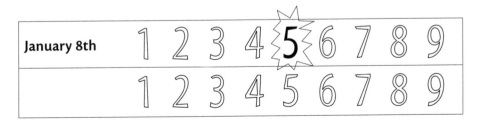

Bar charts

My 'On Task' Chart

Time in minutes	Monday	Tuesday	Wednesday	Thursday	Friday
90					
80					
70					
60					
50	▓				
40	▓				
30	▓				
20	▓				
10	▓				

Colour in how long Mrs Stanton said you managed to stay on task in session

Reading progress tapes

Create a tape-recording of the pupil reading, then tape them again at a later date to let them hear their progress. You can ask them to bring a blank tape in from home and clearly label it with their name and date. At the end of the year, play the pupil's very first and last recordings, which is sure to bring a smile to their face! The pupils can also get involved in taping themselves from time to time. Each and every class has a pupil who is a technical genius who can help others to operate the tape recorder if necessary.

Favourite work folders

Create folders where the pupils can choose work to go inside. These are for pieces of work where they feel they have done a good job and have done particularly well with their targets. Get the pupils to decorate the folders in a way that is unique to them.

Weekly target books

I often use A4 paper folded in half with the following sections, filling it in with either smiley faces or ticks and crosses.

Monday			How did I get on today?
Activity	**Target 1** To stay quiet when others are talking and listen with respect.	**Target 2** To keep my hands and feet to myself.	My thoughts and feelings (circle a face and write or draw why you feel that way).
Lesson 1			
Lesson 2			
	Target 1 To stay in the playground and play without fighting.	**Target 2** To put my litter into the bins and not. on the gorund.	
Break			My teacher/mentor's comments:

The Feelings Diary

For a comprehensive photocopiable diary which allows young people to identify and record their feelings each day you might like to use 'The Feelings Diary,' also published by Lucky Duck Publishing. Each page contains illustrations and words for a range of emotions we all experience from time to time. The illustrations are useful as they make the diary accessible even to those who are unable to read the words. It is especially useful for pupils who display emotional or behavioural difficulties, as it allows them to identify and express uncomfortable feelings in a positive way, rather than hurting others or themselves. It also allows them to look back and monitor how many times they have experienced a particular feeling over a period of time and begin to see patterns of behaviour emerge.

References

Brennan, S. (1988) *A Pupil Perspective on Records of Achievement, Research and Consultancy Report no15,* Northern Ireland Council for Educational Research.

Borba, M. & C. (1978) *Self-Esteem: A Classroom Affair,* Winston Press.

Department for Education (2001) *Special Educational Needs Code of Practice,* London, Central Office of Information.

National Childrenren's Bureau, *Working with the Children Act (1989), An Introduction for Practitioners in Education, Health and Social Work,* London, NCB.

OFSTED Report (1999) *The SEN Code of Practice: Three Years On. The contribution of Individual Education Plans to the raising of standards for pupils with special educational needs,* Central Office of Information.

SEN Toolkit, Section 5, *Managing Individual Education Plans (2001)* DfES, Nottinghamshire.

Shotton, G. (2002) *The Feelings Diary,* Lucky Duck Publishing, Bristol.

The Children Act (1989) Guidance and Regulations, DOH 1991, Vol. 6, 6.6.

Individual Education Plans Template Pages CD-ROM

These Pupil Friendly IEP Template Pages are compatible with Word versions 2001 and later. They are presented on the CD-ROM as individual files for a variety of styles. You can choose from dinosaurs, fish, football, animals and cartoon characters, in colour or as black and white line drawings (for colouring in). The files are organised as follows:

PFIEP Animal BW.doc	= animal drawings in black and white
PFIEP Animal.doc	= animal drawings in colour
PFIEP Dinosaur BW.doc	= dinosaur drawings in black and white
PFIEP Dinosaur.doc	= dinosaur drawings in colour
PFIEP Fish BW.doc	= fish drawings in black and white
PFIEP Fish.doc	= fish drawings in colour
PFIEP Football BW.doc	= football drawings in black and white
PFIEP Football.doc	= football drawings in colour
PFIEP Boy comic BW.doc	= boy cartoons in black and white
PFIEP Boy comic.doc	= boy cartoons in colour
PFIEP Girl comic BW.doc	= girl cartoons in black and white
PFIEP Girl comic.doc	= boy cartoons in colour
PFIEP Character BW.doc	= character in black and white
PFIEP Character.doc	= character in colour

To use the Pupil Friendly IEP CD-ROM for PC (Windows)

1 Put the CD-ROM into your CD Drive

2 Open 'My Computer'

3 Find the CD-ROM (usually drive D:) which will be titled **PFIEP Template Pages**

4 Select the file you wish to work from

5 Open this file then 'Save As' to your C: drive under whatever file name you wish to use (you cannot save any changes to these files to the CD-ROM)

6 Fill-in the form as directed in this guide. The table will expand as your typing fills the boxes. This may push the IEP onto two or more pages, depending on the amount of text.

7 To print the IEP, save first then go to 'File' then 'Print'. The IEP is set to print onto A4 landscape.

To use the Pupil Friendly IEP CD-ROM for Macintosh (OS9 and OSX)

1 Put the CD-ROM into your CD Drive

2 Double click on the icon titled **PFIEP Template Pages** on your desktop

3 Select the file you wish to work from

4 Open this file then 'Save As' to your Hard Disk under whatever file name you wish to use (you cannot save any changes to these files to the CD-ROM)

5 Fill-in the form as directed in this guide. The table will expand as your typing fills the boxes. This may push the IEP onto two or more pages, depending on the amount of text.

6 To print the IEP, save first then go to 'File' then 'Print'. The IEP is set to print onto A4 landscape.

Appendix A: example of a completed IEP for learning

My Individual Education Plan

Things I find difficult	My Targets	What do I need to do?	Who's going to help me and when?	How did I get on? review date 19.2.01
Reading and spelling	To read and spell these words: he, put, was, got cross, they, wanted, everyone, in,to, pulled, pushed, made, said, had, it, went.	I will try to learn 3 words per week. When I get home I will either read my book to mum or I will play a game that will help me to learn my words for that week.	Mrs. Stanton will play games with me to help me learn to read and write my words. Mum and dad are going to remind me to make the words using the letters on the fridge as well as putting them on the back of the toilet door.	
Handwriting	To make my writing look neater with no rubbing out and keep all my letters on the line when I write.	Practise my handwriting for 10 minutes each day using that special handwriting book that I like doing. Try really hard to be a bit neater and write on the line when writing in class. Cross out neatly using a ruler. Don't use a rubber.	Mrs. Barnes will give me a sticker each time she spots me taking care with my work.	

This IEP format has been designed especially for the child. The idea is that the child's teacher will spend some time discussing and writing the content in partnership with the child. This will help the child to feel more involved in their education and therefore more motivated to reach the targets they have helped to set for themselves.

Name: Jack Smith
COP stage: Action plus   IEP number: 5
Date: 8th January 2004

IEP agreed by: Class teacher P. Barnes   SENCO: T. Brown
Pupil: J. Smith   Parent/carer: H. Smith
Other(s): M. Stanton

Appendix B: example of a completed IEP for behaviour

My Individual Education Plan

Things I find difficult	My Targets	What do I need to do?	Who's going to help me and when?	How did I get on? review date 19.2.01
Working with other people without annoying them.	To work with Sam and Matthew for 20 minutes 3 times a week without hitting and be nice to them and listen to them.	If I feel angry I will walk away to the library area. I will take some deep breaths and look at my favourite book to help me feel calm again.	Mrs. Stanton will work with us. She will give me a sticker for my chart if I do my target. At the end of the week if I get 5 stickers Mrs. Barnes will give me a certificate, then dad said he would take me to McDonalds.	
Remembering to put my hand up to talk.	To put my hand up every time I want to say something during the first half of the Literacy Hour.	Always sit facing the poster to remind me about putting my hand up. Look at that.	Mrs. Stanton will give me a sticker if I manage to remember for the first half of the Literacy Hour and don't call out.	
Waiting in the line for dinner.	To keep my hands and feet to myself when everyone is waiting in the line.	To tidy the bookcase for Mrs. Barnes and join the dinner line later, so that I won't be tempted to get into any fights in the line.	I can choose one friend to help me tidy the bookcase.	

This IEP format has been designed especially for the child. The idea is that the child's teacher will spend some time discussing and writing the content in partnership with the child. This will help the child to feel more involved in their education and therefore more motivated to reach the targets they have helped to set for themselves.

Name: Jack Smith

COP stage: Action plus   IEP number: 5

Date: 8th January 2004

IEP agreed by: Class teacher P. Barnes   SENCO: T. Brown

Pupil: J. Smith   Parent/carer: H. Smith

Other(s): M. Stanton

My Individual Education Plan

Things I find difficult	My Targets	What do I need to do?	Who's going to help me and when?	How did I get on? review date

This IEP format has been designed especially for the child. The idea is that the child's teacher will spend some time discussing and writing the content in partnership with the child. This will help the child to feel more involved in their education and therefore more motivated to reach the targets they have helped to set for themselves.

Name:

COP stage:

Date:

IEP agreed by:

IEP number:

Pupil:

Other(s):

SENCO:

Parent/carer:

My Individual Education Plan

Things I find difficult	My Targets	What do I need to do?	Who's going to help me and when?	How did I get on? review date

This IEP format has been designed especially for the child. The idea is that the child's teacher will spend some time discussing and writing the content in partnership with the child. This will help the child to feel more involved in their education and therefore more motivated to reach the targets they have helped to set for themselves.

Name:
COP stage:
Date:

IEP number:

IEP agreed by:
Pupil:
Other(s):

SENCO:
Parent/carer:

My Individual Education Plan

Things I find difficult	My Goals	What do I need to do?	Who's going to help me and when?	How did I get on? review date

This IEP format has been designed especially for the child. The idea is that the child's teacher will spend some time discussing and writing the content in partnership with the child. This will help the child to feel more involved in their education and therefore more motivated to reach the targets they have helped to set for themselves.

Name:
COP stage:
Date:

IEP number:

IEP agreed by:
Pupil:
Other(s):

SENCO:
Parent/carer:

My Individual Education Plan

Things I find difficult	My Targets	What do I need to do?	Who's going to help me and when?	How did I get on? review date

This IEP format has been designed especially for the child. The idea is that the child's teacher will spend some time discussing and writing the content in partnership with the child. This will help the child to feel more involved in their education and therefore more motivated to reach the targets they have helped to set for themselves.

Name:

COP stage:

Date:

IEP number:

IEP agreed by:

Pupil:

Other(s):

SENCO:

Parent/carer:

My Individual Education Plan

Things I find difficult	My Targets	What do I need to do?	Who's going to help me and when?	How did I get on? review date

This IEP format has been designed especially for the child. The idea is that the child's teacher will spend some time discussing and writing the content in partnership with the child. This will help the child to feel more involved in their education and therefore more motivated to reach the targets they have helped to set for themselves.

Name:

COP stage:

Date:

IEP number:

IEP agreed by:

Pupil:

Other(s):

SENCO:

Parent/carer:

My Individual Education Plan

Things I find difficult	My Targets	What do I need to do?	Who's going to help me and when?	How did I get on? review date

This IEP format has been designed especially for the child. The idea is that the child's teacher will spend some time discussing and writing the content in partnership with the child. This will help the child to feel more involved in their education and therefore more motivated to reach the targets they have helped to set for themselves.

Name:

COP stage:

Date:

IEP number:

IEP agreed by:
Pupil:
Other(s):

SENCO:
Parent/carer:

My Individual Education Plan

Things I find difficult	My Targets	What do I need to do?	Who's going to help me and when?	How did I get on? review date

This IEP format has been designed especially for the child. The idea is that the child's teacher will spend some time discussing and writing the content in partnership with the child. This will help the child to feel more involved in their education and therefore more motivated to reach the targets they have helped to set for themselves.

Name:

COP stage:

Date:

IEP number:

IEP agreed by:

Pupil:

Other(s):

SENCO:

Parent/carer:

My Individual Education Plan

Things I find difficult	My Goals	What do I need to do?	Who's going to help me and when?	How did I get on?
				review date

This IEP format has been designed especially for the child. The idea is that the child's teacher will spend some time discussing and writing the content in partnership with the child. This will help the child to feel more involved in their education and therefore more motivated to reach the targets they have helped to set for themselves.

Name:

COP stage:

Date:

IEP number:

IEP agreed by:

Pupil:

Other(s):

SENCO:

Parent/carer:

My Individual Education Plan

Things I find difficult	My Targets	What do I need to do?	Who's going to help me and when?	How did I get on?
				review date

This IEP format has been designed especially for the child. The idea is that the child's teacher will spend some time discussing and writing the content in partnership with the child. This will help the child to feel more involved in their education and therefore more motivated to reach the targets they have helped to set for themselves.

Name:

COP stage:

Date:

IEP number:

IEP agreed by:

Pupil:

Other(s):

SENCO:

Parent/carer:

Getting it Right

A Behaviour Curriculum

Julie Casey

The Getting it Right materials provide a motivating, structured and comprehensive programme which aims to offer even the most troubled pupils the opportunity to develop the skills, knowledge, understanding and self-belief which will help them to 'survive' school.

Structured for small group work, the four sections include:

▶ motivating pupils
▶ setting and achieving goals
▶ locus of control
▶ the classroom context.

This resource will be welcomed by all those who work with difficult pupils in assisting their inclusion in mainstream education.

Success into Secondary

supporting transition with Circle Time

Devised by Cherrie Demain & Lorraine Hurst
Developed by Links Education Support Centre, Primary Team

This book is the result of more than 6 years of work in schools in Hertfordshire, helping children make the transition from primary education to the 'big school'.

The six sessions follow a Circle Time approach with follow-up activities. A 'memory map' technique provides a unifying element to the programme.

Issues covered include:

▶ bullying   ▶ the induction day
▶ friendship   ▶ meeting new people

Children's comments include:

"Many of the worries I had are now gone and I can't wait for secondary school." Eleanor

"Helped me with confidence and facing my fears such as bullying." Daniel.

An interactive and fun approach to assist Year 6 pupils make a successful transition.

1 873 942 34 6	£24.00	ages 11 to 16
Copiable teaching resource		4 units

1 904 315 28 3	£14.00	ages 10 to 11
Book and CD-ROM		10 sessions

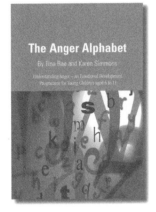

Crucial Skills

An Anger Management and Problem
Solving Teaching Programme for High
School Students

Penny Johnson and Tina Rae

This programme is aimed at students (aged
11 to 16) with challenging and angry behaviours leading to disaffection and disciplinary
problems. The handbook includes teacher
notes, lesson plans and photocopiable
resources.

The 10 lessons and follow up work empower
students to:

- ▶ reflect on behaviour and consequences
- ▶ recognise and understand feelings
- ▶ develop strategies to control angry
  outbursts
- ▶ respond to conflict without anger
- ▶ resolve relationship difficulties.

The programme promotes self-belief in students that they can effect change in their
behaviour and achieve a positive outcome to
reduce the risk of exclusion.

1 873 942 67 2	£20.00	ages 11 to 16
Copiable teaching resource		10 sessions

Anger Alphabet

Understanding Anger
An Emotional Development Programme
for Young Children

Tina Rae and Karen Simmons

The 26 elements of this programme help children understand anger and to see that it is
linked with other feelings such as fear, loss
and jealousy etc. They will begin to realise
that anger is not always harmful and negative
but should be managed effectively.

There are complete teacher instructions,
including discussion, Circle Time activities,
photocopiable posters and worksheets, and
ideas for plenary and follow-up work.

At the end of the programme pupils will:

- ▶ distinguish between behaviours
- ▶ develop anger management strategies
- ▶ express strong feelings in an assertive way
- ▶ learn to recognise anger in its early stages
- ▶ develop an understanding of
  others' perspectives.

1 873 942 69 9	£18.00	ages 6 to 11
Copiable teaching resource		26 sessions